"I think I'm having a relationship with a blueberry pie!"

A Cathy Book
by Cathy Guisewite

The Cathy Chronicles Volume 2

BANTAM BOOKS
TORONTO · NEW YORK · LONDON · SYDNEY

"I THINK I'M HAVING A RELATIONSHIP
WITH A BLUEBERRY PIE!"
A Bantam Book/published by arrangement with
Andrews & McMeel Inc.

PRINTING HISTORY
Andrews & McMeel edition
published November 1978
Bantam edition/September 1981

ISBN 0-553-01337-8

Library of Congress Catalog Card No. 81-43096

Published simultaneously in the
United States and Canada

Bantam Books are published by Bantam Books, Inc. Its
trademark, consisting of the words "Bantam Books"
and the portrayal of a bantam, is Registered in U.S. Pat-
ent and Trademark Office and in other countries. Marca
Registrada, Bantam Books, Inc., 666 Fifth Avenue, New
York, New York 10103.

PRINTED IN THE UNITED STATES OF AMERICA

0 9 8 7 6 5 4 3 2 1

To mom and dad,
who made both
cathys possible.

My parents are the kind of people who go around telling you to be grateful for everything that goes wrong in your life. Every big crisis has a purpose, they say. Every little disappointment, a bright and wonderful side.

Having grown up being forced to look for the good side of the worst moments of my life, I found that *Cathy* came about in a very natural way.

Instead of wallowing in the misery of waiting for phone calls that never came a few years ago, I was compelled to draw a picture of me waiting. . . .

Instead of agonizing over where love had gone, I couldn't resist putting my questions down on paper. . . .

And when I was filled with the drive to make radical changes in the way I was living, I couldn't help visualizing my determination. . . .

Although I never suspected I was creating a comic strip, *Cathy's* beginnings were in drawings just like these. They became a great release for my frustrations, and by sending them home, I discovered a great way to let my family know how I was doing without writing letters.

Anxious to have me do even better, my parents researched comic strip syndicates, sought advice from Tom Wilson, the creator of *Ziggy*, and, finally, threatened to send my work to Universal Press Syndicate if I didn't.

Just as Cathy began as a kind of self-therapy for my problems, she continues to be a voice for the questions I can never quite answer, and the things I can never quite say. Because our lives are linked so closely, she's affected by almost everyone I know and everything I do.

The strips in this book are arranged pretty much in the order that they first appeared in the newspaper. No doubt you'll notice that Cathy looks a little different toward the end of the book than she does in the first pages. But you'll also see a difference in her attitudes and relationships that are simply a reflection of the fact that in the last two years, I've changed too.

In this way, I want to always keep Cathy very real to life. Through her, I've learned that my little daily struggles are a lot like everyone else's little daily struggles. The feelings I always thought that only I had are ones that everyone shares. But maybe just as important, writing Cathy has taught me one of the even greater lessons of life: anything is possible if you listen to your mother.

THIS OUTFIT MIGHT BE CUTE FOR THE OFFICE ONCE IT'S IRONED.

OH NO, MISS. THE LOOK FOR SPRING IS ALL RUMPLED AND WRINKLED.

YOU'RE **SUPPOSED** TO LOOK LIKE YOU SLEPT IN IT.

THAT'S RIDICULOUS.

I MIGHT AS WELL GO TO WORK IN A PAIR OF PAJAMAS!!

DON'T BE SILLY.

ALL OUR SLEEPWEAR IS PERMANENT PRESS.

HOW'S THIS?

WELL, IT'S NICE FOR STARTERS... BUT THE LOOK FOR SPRING IS LAYERED.

YOU WEAR T-SHIRTS ON TOP OF T-SHIRTS... ...BLOUSES ON TOP OF BLOUSES!

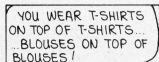

SKIRTS ON TOP OF SKIRTS! VESTS ON TOP OF VESTS!! JACKETS ON TOP OF EVERYTHING!!

CONGRATULATIONS.

YOU JUST TURNED MY ENTIRE SPRING WARDROBE INTO ONE OUTFIT.

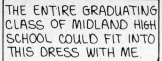

11

WHEN I SEE THESE NEW RUFFLED BLOUSES ON TV, THE GIRLS LOOK SOFT AND SEXY.

WHEN I SEE THESE NEW RUFFLED SKIRTS IN THE MAGAZINES, THE MODELS LOOK SULTRY AND ALLURING.

I JUST DON'T UNDERSTAND IT, ANDREA.

NO MATTER WHAT I PUT ON, I LOOK LIKE LITTLE BO PEEP.

LET'S SEE...450 CALORIES FOR A STEAK...138 FOR THE VEGETABLE...157 FOR MILK...

WELL, I'M GLAD YOU'RE STARTING TO EAT SENSIBLE DINNERS ON YOUR DIET, CATHY.

NO, I'M NOT, ANDREA.

I'M JUST HAVING A PIECE OF CHOCOLATE CAKE.

THEN WHY ARE YOU ADDING UP ALL THIS OTHER STUFF ??

I'M TRYING TO FIGURE OUT HOW MANY CALORIES I'M SAVING BY EATING SOMETHING FATTENING.

12

SUPER GLOSS EYE SHADOW...

WONDER GLOSS BLUSH-ON... GLOSSIEST GLOSS LIP GLOSS...

AREN'T YOU READY YET, CATHY?

NOT QUITE, IRVING.

I HAVE TO POWDER MY SHINY NOSE.

IT'S HARD BEING SINGLE TODAY, MOM. THERE AREN'T ANY RULES.

I MEAN, EVERY GIRL REALLY HAS TO SET UP AND LIVE BY HER OWN MORAL CODE.

WHAT'S SO HARD ABOUT THAT?

YOU DATE A NICE BOY, YOU FALL IN LOVE, YOU GET MARRIED.

SELECTING YOUR MORAL CODE ALWAYS SEEMS LIKE A BIGGER PROBLEM WHEN YOUR MOTHER ISN'T IN THE ROOM.

13

14

YOU'RE EATING FRENCH FRIES WITH YOUR HAMBURGER, CATHY! I THOUGHT YOU WERE ON A DIET!

IT'S OKAY, ANDREA. I'M NOT GOING TO EAT THE BUN.

A MILKSHAKE, TOO?!

ANDREA, I TOLD YOU. I'M NOT TOUCHING THE BUN.

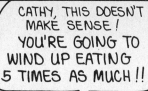

CATHY, THIS DOESN'T MAKE SENSE! YOU'RE GOING TO WIND UP EATING 5 TIMES AS MUCH!!

NEVER EXPECT A SKINNY PERSON TO UNDERSTAND THE SIGNIFICANCE OF NOT EATING THE BUN.

YOU KNOW WHY YOUR DIETS ALWAYS FAIL, CATHY? YOU FORGET ALL ABOUT TRYING TO LEARN TO EAT RIGHT. YOU FORGET THAT YOU'RE SUPPOSED TO BE RE-EDUCATING YOUR EATING HABITS!

YOU FORGET WHAT YOUR GOAL REALLY IS!!

I KNOW WHAT MY GOAL IS, ANDREA.

I WANT TO GET SO SKINNY THAT PEOPLE WILL BEG ME TO EAT.

AND THEN WHAT?

THEN I'LL EAT!!

15

WITH PERSEVERANCE AND DEDICATION, YOU CAN HAVE ANYTHING IN THE WORLD YOU WANT, CATHY.

RIGHT ON, ANDREA!

WITH STAMINA AND WILL POWER, YOU CAN HAVE ANYTHING YOU WANT!

RIGHT ON!!

WITH POSITIVE THINKING AND DETERMINATION, YOU CAN HAVE ANYTHING YOU WANT!!

RIGHT ON! RIGHT ON!! RIGHT ON!!!

HOW AM I SUPPOSED TO FIGURE OUT WHAT I WANT?

HI I'D LIKE MY MONEY BACK FOR THIS DEODORANT.

WHAT'S THE MATTER WITH IT? DON'T YOU LIKE THE NEW NATURAL SCENT?

IF I LIKED THE NATURAL SCENT, I WOULDN'T HAVE BEEN BUYING DEODORANT IN THE FIRST PLACE.

TRUST IS KNOWING THAT THE COMPANY YOU'RE HAVING WON'T PEEK BEHIND THE SHOWER CURTAIN TO SEE IF YOU'VE CLEANED THE BATHTUB RECENTLY.

WHY AREN'T YOU TALKING TO ME, IRVING? IS IT SOMETHING I SAID? IS IT SOMETHING I DID??

IS IT OVER BETWEEN US, IRVING?? WHAT HAPPENED?? WHAT WENT WRONG?? WHY ARE YOU BEING LIKE THIS??!!

I GOT MY HAIR CUT TODAY AND THE BARBER MADE IT TOO SHORT.

IT'S JUST LIKE A MAN TO BLAME EVERYTHING ON HIS HAIR.

I DON'T GET IT, IRVING. IF MY HAIR DOESN'T TURN OUT RIGHT ONE DAY AND I WANT TO SPEND 5 EXTRA MINUTES FIXING IT BEFORE WE GO OUT, YOU GO BERSERK.

BUT YOU SEE NOTHING WRONG WITH MOPING AROUND ABOUT YOUR STUPID HAIRCUT FOR AN ENTIRE WEEK !!

WHAT'S THE BIG DIFFERENCE ??!

IT'S **MY** HAIR !!!

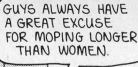

GUYS ALWAYS HAVE A GREAT EXCUSE FOR MOPING LONGER THAN WOMEN.

YOUR HAIRCUT IS CUTE, IRVING

CUTE ?? THE BARBER SCALPED ME !!

I THINK IT'S CUTE.

CATHY, EVEN IF HE'D GIVEN ME THE GREATEST HAIRCUT IN THE WORLD, **CUTE** ISN'T THE WORD YOU SHOULD USE TO DESCRIBE IT!

NO GUY WANTS TO BE TOLD HE HAS **CUTE** HAIR !! WE HATE CUTE !!!

IT LOOKS EVEN CUTER WHEN YOUR FACE TURNS PURPLE LIKE THAT.

AAAUGH!!

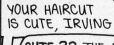

21

I SAVED 2½ HOURS BY MAKING A FROZEN TV DINNER INSTEAD OF A REGULAR MEAL...

I SAVED 45 MINUTES BY SPEED READING THE NEWSPAPER...I SAVED AN HOUR BY CLEANING UP WITH PRESTO POLISH...

FOR A TOTAL SAVINGS THIS EVENING OF 4 HOURS AND 15 MINUTES... ...MULTIPLIED BY THE MINIMUM WAGE OF $2.65 AN HOUR....

SOMEBODY OWES ME $11.26.

IT ISN'T FAIR, ANDREA. I CAN'T TALK TO YOU ABOUT MY RELATIONSHIP WITH IRVING BECAUSE YOU JUST TELL ME WHAT A JERK I AM FOR STILL SEEING HIM.

I CAN'T TALK TO MY MOM BECAUSE SHE JUST SAYS I'LL NEVER GET MARRIED UNLESS I TRY TO MEET SOME NEW GUYS...WHO AM I SUPPOSED TO TALK TO?!

TO **IRVING**, CATHY. YOU SHOULD BE TALKING ABOUT YOUR RELATION- SHIP **WITH IRVING** !

FORGET IT, ANDREA.

HE WON'T TAKE MY SIDE, EITHER.

23

LOOK AT ALL THESE NEW SUMMER CLASSES, CATHY. THERE ARE SELF-AWARENESS GROUPS TO HELP YOU DISCOVER WHO YOU REALLY ARE...

ENCOUNTER GROUPS, TO HELP YOU DEAL WITH WHO YOU REALLY ARE...

ASSERTIVENESS TRAINING GROUPS TO HELP YOU STAND UP FOR WHO YOU REALLY ARE...

SUDDENLY, THE ONLY WAY TO BECOME AN INDIVIDUAL IS TO JOIN A GROUP.

WHEN YOU'RE OLDER, YOU'LL LAUGH ABOUT ALL THIS, CATHY.

I KNOW, MOM.

WHEN YOU'RE OLDER, YOU'LL LAUGH ABOUT EVERYTHING YOU THINK IS SUCH A BIG PROBLEM.

I KNOW.

BUT IT JUST DOESN'T SEEM FAIR THAT I SHOULD HAVE TO WAIT FOR 10 YEARS TO SEE WHAT'S SO FUNNY.

NOW IS WHEN I NEED THE CHEERING UP.

Panel 1: WELL, HERE I AM. YOUNG, SINGLE AND FREE.

Panel 2: WITH THE EARTH AT MY FEET AND THE WORLD AT MY FINGERTIPS!!

Panel 3: IF I COULD ONLY FIGURE OUT WHAT TO DO WITH THE REST OF ME, I'D BE PERFECT.

Guisewite

Panel 4: I'M PROUD TO SEE THAT YOU'RE DOING YOUR OWN INCOME TAXES THIS YEAR, CATHY.

Panel 5: IT'S SO IMPORTANT TO PROVE THAT WE WOMEN ARE CAPABLE OF TAKING CHARGE OF OUR OWN FINANCES!!

Panel 6: I KNOW. I'VE BEEN WORKING ON MY TAXES FOR 2 HOURS ALREADY.

GREAT! HOW ARE YOU COMING?

Panel 7: SO FAR, I'VE GOT MY NAME AND ADDRESS FILLED IN.

Panel 1: BUT CATHY, I THOUGHT YOU WERE GOING TO DO YOUR **OWN** TAXES.

I WAS, ANDREA.

Panel 2: I COLLECTED DOCUMENTED EVIDENCE TO PROVE THAT EVERY ENTRY IS LEGAL... I HAVE EVERY TEENY SALES SLIP TO PROVE THAT EVERY DEDUCTION IS HONEST...

Panel 3: I HAVE CANCELLED CHECKS AND NOTARIZED RECEIPTS TO PROVE THAT EVERY TRANSACTION OF MY LIFE HAS BEEN ABOVE BOARD.

SO WHY DO YOU NEED AN ACCOUNTANT??

Panel 4: TO HELP ME FIGURE OUT HOW TO CHEAT.

Panel 5: I GO TO WORK, I COME HOME FROM WORK... I GO TO WORK, I COME HOME FROM WORK...

Panel 6: FOR WHAT??

CATHY, THIS ISN'T JUST WORK. YOU'RE LIVING OUT THE NEW WOMAN'S DREAM! YOU'RE MAKING SOMETHING OF YOURSELF!!

Panel 7: THIS IS YOUR FUTURE!! THIS IS YOUR **CAREER**!!

I SEE WHAT YOU MEAN, ANDREA.

Panel 8: I GO TO MY CAREER, I COME HOME FROM MY CAREER... I GO TO MY CAREER, I COME HOME FROM MY CAREER...

27

28

IRVING, DO YOU FEEL CLOSER TO ME NOW THAN YOU DID ON OUR FIRST DATE?

SURE I DO, CATHY.

DO YOU FEEL CLOSER TO ME THAN YOU DID WHEN WE'D KNOWN EACH OTHER FOR A MONTH?

OF COURSE.

DO YOU THINK WE'RE CLOSER NOW THAN WE'VE EVER BEEN BEFORE?

NO QUESTION ABOUT IT.

THE CLOSER WE GET, THE FARTHER APART WE SIT.

I'M GETTING OLD, MOM.

DON'T BE SILLY, CATHY. YOU'RE A YOUNG WOMAN.

WELL, I THOUGHT SO. BUT WHEN I SEE MYSELF IN THE MIRROR, I DON'T LOOK LIKE I USED TO.

THAT'S ONLY NATURAL, CATHY.

BUT ONE LITTLE CHANGE OR TWO DOESN'T MEAN YOU'RE GETTING OLD.

I THINK IT'S MORE SERIOUS THAN THAT, MOM.

THIS MORNING I DIDN'T RECOGNIZE MY LEGS.

29

WHAT DO WE HAVE TO BE SO INDEPENDENT FOR, ANDREA?

WE JUST DO, CATHY.

WHEN A WOMAN IS FINANCIALLY AND EMOTIONALLY INDEPENDENT, HER LIFE WILL NEVER FALL APART IF ALL OF THE SUDDEN THERE ISN'T A MAN IN IT ANYMORE.

WHAT'S THE DIFFERENCE?

WOMEN'S STUDIES

MY LIFE FALLS APART WHEN THERE **IS** A MAN IN IT.

I SEE YOU'RE SCOTCH-TAPING YOUR BATHING SUIT TO THE REFRIGERATOR AGAIN, CATHY.

YES, ANDREA.

IT'S THE SUMMER DIET INCENTIVE RITUAL I LEARNED FROM MY FRIEND, CHRIS.

BUT, CATHY, IT NEVER WORKS!!

SURE IT DOES, ANDREA.

AS LONG AS MY BATHING SUIT IS STUCK TO THE REFRIGERATOR, I HAVE AN EXCUSE FOR NOT PUTTING IT ON.

33

I THOUGHT WE AGREED ON NO MORE SURPRISE VISITS, MOM.

REMEMBER? WE DECIDED THAT SINCE I'M A GROWN WOMAN WITH A PLACE OF MY OWN, YOU SHOULD RESPECT MY PRIVACY LIKE YOU WOULD ANY ADULT'S.

BUT SWEETIE, I DO RESPECT YOUR PRIVACY.

IF YOU HAVE SOMETHING TO HIDE, I'LL JUST STAND OUT HERE IN THE HALL.

I THOUGHT YOU SAID YOU DIDN'T GO OUT LAST NIGHT, IRVING.

OF COURSE I DIDN'T GO OUT, CATHY. I WAS RIGHT HERE.

HEH... WHAT MAKES YOU THINK I WASN'T RIGHT HERE??

YOUR TV GUIDE IS STILL CREASED OPEN TO TUESDAY.

34

36

38

39

OF COURSE I KNOW THAT IRVING CARES ABOUT ME, ANDREA.

HOW DO YOU KNOW, CATHY?

I CAN SEE IT IN HIS EYES.

HOW CAN YOU SEE IT IN HIS EYES?? HALF THE TIME YOU'RE WITH HIM HE'S ASLEEP IN FRONT OF THE TV SET!!

I CAN SEE IT IN HIS EYELIDS.

HI. I'D LIKE TO RETURN THIS HAIRDRYER. I'VE ONLY HAD IT FOR 6 MONTHS AND IT QUIT WORKING.

I'M SORRY, MISS...

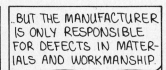

..BUT THE MANUFACTURER IS ONLY RESPONSIBLE FOR DEFECTS IN MATERIALS AND WORKMANSHIP.

ISN'T IT A DEFECT IF A $25 HAIRDRYER POOPS OUT IN 6 MONTHS??!

GOODNESS NO. OUR DRYERS LAST MUCH LONGER IF GIVEN THE PROPER CARE.

WHAT WAS I SUPPOSED TO DO?!

ONLY WASH YOUR HAIR ONCE A MONTH.

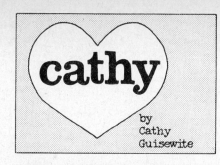

41

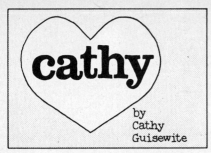

cathy

by Cathy Guisewite

YOU'RE NOT MAKING ANOTHER ROOT BEER FLOAT, ARE YOU??

I HAVE TO. I'M FRUSTRATED.

BUT THAT'S ALL WRONG.

CATHY, THE WHOLE KEY TO BECOMING A MORE ASSERTIVE, INDEPENDENT HUMAN BEING IS LEARNING TO EXPRESS HOW YOU FEEL IN **WORDS**!!

WHEN YOU'RE FRUSTRATED, EXPLAIN **WHY** YOU'RE FRUSTRATED! DON'T DUMP ROOT BEER FLOATS ON YOUR FEELINGS!!

WHEN YOU'RE MAD, YELL AND SCREAM AND **SAY** YOU'RE MAD! DON'T SUFFOCATE YOUR ANGER WITH A BIG MAC!!

WHEN YOU'RE HAPPY, **BE** HAPPY! DON'T CELEBRATE WITH HOSTESS CUPCAKES AND MALTED MILK BALLS!!

JUST ONE QUESTION, ANDREA.

WHEN DO I GET TO **EAT**?!!!

42

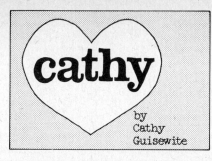

cathy

by Cathy Guisewite

"MIX INGREDIENTS IN BLENDER FOR 30 SECONDS, OR BY HAND FOR 45 MINUTES..."

DIAL, DIAL, DIAL.

HI, MOM. I'M HAVING SOME FRIENDS OVER FOR SUPPER TONIGHT. CAN I BORROW YOUR BLENDER?

SURE, CATHY... OF COURSE, IF YOU GOT MARRIED, YOU'D HAVE A SHOWER, AND YOU'D GET A BLENDER OF YOUR OWN.

COULD I ALSO BORROW YOUR MUFFIN TINS AND YOUR GOOD STEAK KNIVES?

SURE... OF COURSE, IF YOU GOT MARRIED AND HAD A SHOWER, YOU'D HAVE THOSE TOO.

HOW ABOUT YOUR ELECTRIC CAN OPENER?

YOU'D PROBABLY HAVE 3 OR 4 OF THOSE IF YOU GOT MARRIED AND HAD A SHOWER.

C'MON, MOM...THAT'S NOT FAIR! WHY SHOULD I HAVE TO GET MARRIED AND HAVE A SHOWER BEFORE I GET ALL THE STUFF I NEED?!?!!

WE DON'T WANT YOU TO GET TOO COMFORTABLE BEING SINGLE.

43

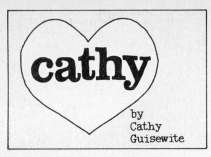

cathy

by Cathy Guisewite

IRVING?... IRVING??

WAKE UP, IRVING!

I'VE BEEN READING ABOUT ALL THESE MARRIAGE CONTRACTS AND LIVING TOGETHER CONTRACTS, IRVING, AND I'VE BEEN THINKING...

I THINK WE SHOULD WRITE UP A DATING CONTRACT.

WHAT, ARE YOU CRAZY?

NO. IT MAKES SENSE, IRVING. THAT WAY EACH ONE OF US WILL KNOW JUST WHAT IS EXPECTED OF EACH OTHER IN THE RELATIONSHIP.

SEE? I'VE WRITTEN DOWN HERE THAT I EXPECT YOU TO SPEND 3 EVENINGS A WEEK WITH ME, PLUS SATURDAYS... TO CALL WHEN YOU SAY YOU'RE GOING TO... TO PAY FOR ALL MOVIES... ...AND TO BE SWEET AND THOUGHTFUL AT ALL TIMES.

NOW, WHAT DO YOU EXPECT FROM ME?

I THINK I BETTER CALL MY LAWYER.

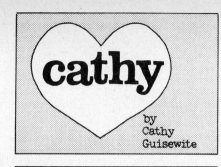

cathy
by Cathy Guisewite

"ARE YOU HEADED FOR PARADISE OR THE PITS?"

HEY, LOOK AT THIS!

IRVING, I FOUND A NEW COMPATIBILITY TEST FOR US TO TAKE IN THIS MAGAZINE

NO, CATHY... DO WE HAVE TO ??

YES... "QUESTION 1: IN CASE OF FIRE, WHAT WOULD YOU TRY TO SAVE FIRST...
A) THE TV SET.
B) YOUR BOWLING TROPHIES.
C) THE SCARF AND MITTEN SET YOUR MOTHER MADE YOU."

"QUESTION 2: IF SOMEONE HANDED YOU $5,000,000.00, YOU WOULD...
A) BUY YOURSELF THE MOST HIDEOUSLY EXPENSIVE GIFTS YOU CAN FIND.
B) FIGURE OUT HOW TO CHEAT ON YOUR INCOME TAY.
C) GET SOME NEW YARN FOR YOUR MOM."

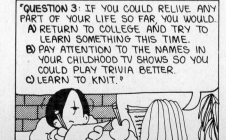

"QUESTION 3: IF YOU COULD RELIVE ANY PART OF YOUR LIFE SO FAR, YOU WOULD...
A) RETURN TO COLLEGE AND TRY TO LEARN SOMETHING THIS TIME.
B) PAY ATTENTION TO THE NAMES IN YOUR CHILDHOOD TV SHOWS SO YOU COULD PLAY TRIVIA BETTER.
C) LEARN TO KNIT."

HOW ARE WE DOING?

WELL, I'LL JUST ADD UP OUR SCORES AND....

SO FAR, YOUR MOTHER AND I MAKE THE PERFECT COUPLE.

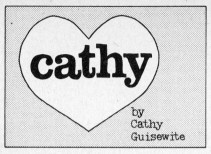

cathy

by Cathy Guisewite

"CUPCAKES SO EASY, A CHILD CAN MAKE THEM...."

"SALAD DRESSING SO CREAMY, IT TASTES LIKE YOU MADE IT YOURSELF...."

"SOUP JUST LIKE YOUR MOM USED TO MAKE..."

"GRAVY LIKE GRANDMA USED TO MAKE...."

"LEMONADE LIKE GRANDPA HAD WHEN HE WAS A BOY...."

"CINNAMON ROLLS EVEN A FATHER CAN BAKE...."

AT LAST. I'VE GOT THE WHOLE FAMILY TOGETHER FOR A MEAL.

46

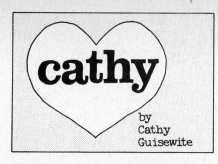

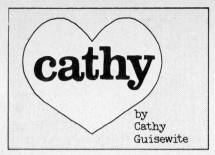

49

50

EXCUSE ME, SIR. DO YOU SUPPORT THE E.R.A.?

ERA TODAY

YES.

ERA TODAY! NOW NOW!

WO ERA ERA

THESE ARE COOKIES MADE FROM THE NEW COOKIE MIX I WANT YOU TO TEST THIS WEEK, CATHY.

UCT TESTING, INC

YECHH! THESE TASTE TERRIBLE, MR. PINKLEY!

NO THEY DON'T, CATHY. THEY TASTE LIKE HOMEMADE.

PRODUCT TESTING,

SEE? IT SAYS IT RIGHT ON THE BOX.

I'M SORRY, BUT THE COOKIES I MAKE NEVER TASTED LIKE THIS.

PRODUCT TESTING

HM. MAYBE YOU'VE BEEN LEAVING OUT THE PROPYLENE GLYCOL.

PRODUCT TEST

51

HI, JODY. FOR OUR TEST TODAY, I WANT YOU TO EAT THIS COOKIE MADE FROM A COOKIE MIX AND TELL ME IF IT TASTES LIKE HOMEMADE.

NOPE.

MR. PINKLEY, COME QUICK!! I **KNEW** I'D FIND A CHILD WHOSE MOTHER DOESN'T MAKE COOKIES FROM A BOX!!

MY MOM MAKES THE KIND THAT COME IN A TUBE.

NOT ONE OF THE KIDS I TESTED AT WORK TODAY HAD EVER TASTED A REAL CHOCOLATE CHIP COOKIE BEFORE, ANDREA!

THAT DOESN'T MEAN THEY'RE DEPRIVED, CATHY.

THEY'RE GROWING UP IN HOMES WHERE THE MOTHERS THINK THERE ARE MORE IMPORTANT THINGS TO DO THAN BAKE ALL DAY.

THESE KIDS ARE EXPERIENCING A **LIBER-ATED HOME**, CATHY! THEY'RE EXPERIENCING A **WHOLE NEW WAY OF LIFE!!**

WHAT IS LIFE WITHOUT REAL CHOCOLATE CHIP COOKIES?

52

 AACK! THE COKE'S COMING OUT BUT THERE ISN'T A CUP THERE!!!

OH, THAT'S RIGHT. WE WON'T BE GETTING OUR CUP SHIPMENT FOR A COUPLE OF WEEKS.

 WHAT AM I SUPPOSED TO DO? STICK MY HEAD UNDER THE SQUIRTER?? WHY WOULD YOU WANT TO DO THAT, LADY?

 YOUR COKE ALREADY RAN DOWN THE DRAIN.

 WAIT A MINUTE. THERE'S NO HANDLE ON THE SNICKER'S BAR SLOT!!

 GIVE ME BACK MY MONEY, YOU STUPID MACHINE!!! FORGET IT, CATHY. THAT MACHINE NEVER WORKS.

 WELL, HOW ARE YOU SUPPOSED TO GET YOUR MONEY BACK?? YOU CAN'T.

 BUT YOU'LL FEEL BETTER IF YOU RIP OFF A HANDLE

54

MAKE ANOTHER SELECTION? WHAT FOR?? I CAN SEE THAT LAST BOX OF MILK DUDS IN THERE!!

GIVE ME THAT BOX OF MILK DUDS!!!

LADY, THE MACHINE CAN'T SELL YOU THE LAST PACK OF CANDY.

WHY NOT??!

HOW WOULD YOU KNOW WHAT YOUR SELECTION IS?

YOU'VE BEEN TRYING TO MAKE THAT CANDY MACHINE WORK FOR HALF AN HOUR, CATHY.

WHY DON'T YOU GIVE UP?

AHAH!!

SEE ALEX? YOU JUST HAVE TO BE PATIENT.

YOU ALSO HAVE TO BE WILLING TO PAY $4.50 FOR A ROLL OF LIFESAVERS.

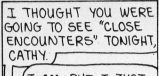

I THOUGHT YOU WERE GOING TO SEE "CLOSE ENCOUNTERS" TONIGHT, CATHY.

I AM... BUT I JUST HAVE TO READ THIS REVIEW OF IT FIRST.

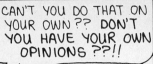

FOR WHAT??

I WANT TO MAKE SURE I HAVE SOMETHING WITTY TO SAY WHEN I WALK OUT OF THE MOVIE.

CAN'T YOU DO THAT ON YOUR OWN?? DON'T YOU HAVE YOUR OWN OPINIONS??!!

OF COURSE I DO, ANDREA.

I'M JUST ALWAYS MORE SURE OF MY OPINIONS IF I'VE READ THEM IN THE NEWSPAPER FIRST.

EXCUSE ME, MISS, BUT I NOTICED THAT THIS ONE BOTTLE OF HAIR CONDITIONER COSTS $7, AND THIS OTHER ONE ONLY COSTS 29¢.

COULD YOU TELL ME WHAT THE BIG DIFFERENCE IS?

CERTAINLY.

THE $7 BOTTLE IS SMALLER.

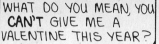

WHAT DO YOU MEAN, YOU **CAN'T** GIVE ME A VALENTINE THIS YEAR?

LOOK, CATHY, CAN I HELP IT IF I'M A TOUGH, MACHO GUY INCAPABLE OF DISPLAYING EMOTION?

YOU DIDN'T HAVE ANY TROUBLE DISPLAYING EMOTION TO THAT LITTLE CHICK AT THE MOVIES LAST WEEK!

YOU DIDN'T HAVE ANY TROUBLE DISPLAYING EMOTION TO THE WAITRESS AT THE EGG PALACE LAST NIGHT!!

BUT CATHY, I DIDN'T EVEN **KNOW** THOSE GIRLS.

SO WHAT??!!

GUYS ALWAYS FIND IT EASIER TO GET EMOTIONAL WITH STRANGERS.

YOU DON'T UNDERSTAND THE MALE PSYCHE, CATHY. IT'S EMBARRASSING FOR A GUY TO STAND IN THE STORE READING VALENTINE'S DAY CARDS.

IT'S HUMILIATING TO WAIT IN THE CHECK OUT LINE WITH A BOX OF CANDY COVERED WITH HEARTS AND LACE UNDER MY ARM... I FEEL STUPID TRYING TO PICK OUT FLOWERS!!

GUYS DON'T KNOW ANYTHING ABOUT THIS JUNK, CATHY!!

IRVING, HOW DO YOU THINK THE OTHER 2 BILLION MEN IN THE WORLD GIVE VALENTINES??

MAYBE THEY HAVE THEIR GIRLFRIENDS PICK THEM OUT.

57

IRVING ISN'T GOING TO GIVE ME A VALENTINE AGAIN THIS YEAR, ANDREA.

SO WHAT?

NOBODY IN THE WORLD MAKES AS BIG A DEAL ABOUT VALENTINE'S DAY AS YOU DO, CATHY.

YEAH, BUT HE ISN'T GOING TO DO IT JUST BECAUSE HE'S EMBARRASSED TO SHOW THAT HE CARES.

CATHY, IF YOU ALREADY **KNOW** HE CARES, WHAT DIFFERENCE DOES IT MAKE IF HE SENDS YOU A VALENTINE OR NOT?

IT'S MY ONE BIG CHANCE IN THE YEAR TO SEE IT IN WRITING.

Guisewite

YOU **FORGOT** THAT TODAY IS VALENTINE'S DAY ?!!! IRVING, WE'VE DISCUSSED THIS **EVERY** DAY FOR A MONTH!!!

EVERY DRUG STORE, CANDY STORE, FLOWER STORE AND JEWELRY STORE IN AMERICA HAS VALENTINE'S DAY PLASTERED ACROSS ITS WINDOWS!!

THE TV SPECIALS SAY VALENTINES!! THE MAGAZINES ALL SAY VALENTINES!! **IT IS NOT POSSIBLE TO...**

OKAY, OKAY. I REMEMBERED.

HAPPY VALENTINE'S DAY.

Guisewite

LOOK AT THIS, ALEX. I'VE USED THE CORRECT CHANGE... I HAVE NOT USED FOREIGN MONEY...

I'VE WAITED FOR EACH COIN TO DROP BEFORE DEPOSITING THE NEXT... ...AND I STILL CAN'T GET ANY CANDY OUT!

WELL, THERE'S ONLY ONE EXPLANATION, CATHY.

I KNOW.

THIS MACHINE IS IN CAHOOTS WITH MY MOTHER.

HELLO CATHY, MY SWEET. I JUST CALLED TO BEG YOU TO BE MY VALENTINE THIS YEAR.

EMERSON... YOU KNOW MY HEART BELONGS TO IRVING.

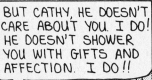

BUT CATHY, HE DOESN'T CARE ABOUT YOU. I DO! HE DOESN'T SHOWER YOU WITH GIFTS AND AFFECTION. I DO!!

THERE'S NO LOGIC HERE!!

YES THERE IS.

MY HEART ALWAYS BELONGS TO THE ONE WHO DOESN'T WANT IT.

60

WHY DON'T YOU TAKE ONE OF THESE BAHAMA VACATION TRIPS, CATHY? YOU COULD USE A BREAK.

I CAN'T. IRVING DOESN'T GET A VACATION UNTIL JULY.

SO, GO BY YOURSELF! WOMEN TODAY DON'T NEED TO HAVE THEIR BOYFRIENDS CHAUFFEUR THEM ALL OVER THE PLACE... WE DON'T NEED HUSBANDS TO PROTECT US AND PAY OUR WAYS!!

MILLIONS OF WOMEN ARE DISCOVERING THE JOYS OF TRAVELLING ALONE THESE DAYS!!

I KNOW.

THEY'RE ALL LOOKING FOR NEW BOYFRIENDS AND HUSBANDS.

HI. I'D LIKE TO FIND OUT ABOUT YOUR $169 ROUND TRIP 7-DAY WHIRLWIND TOUR TO THE BAHAMAS. DOES THAT PRICE INCLUDE AIR FARE?

OH MY NO. AIR FARE IS ON TOP OF THAT.

I SEE. IT JUST COVERS THE HOTELS AND MEALS?

OH NO. HOTELS AND MEALS ARE EXTRA.

TRAVEL-BES

THE $169 SIMPLY COVERS OUR SERVICES.

FOR WHAT??

WE TELL YOU HOW MUCH EVERYTHING ELSE COSTS.

TRAVEL-BEST

Panel 1: OH CATHY. LOOK AT THIS CUTE LITTLE GRASS HUT HOTEL. IS THAT WHERE YOU'RE STAYING IN THE BAHAMAS?

Panel 2: NO, ANDREA. THE HOLIDAY INN.

THE WHAT?!!

Panel 3: CATHY, THIS IS YOUR BIG CHANCE TO EXPERIENCE SOMETHING DIFFERENT! ...TO FEEL THE COMFORTS OF A TOTALLY FOREIGN WAY OF LIFE!

FORGET IT, ANDREA.

Panel 4: I CAN'T FEEL COMFORTABLE UNLESS I'M SURROUNDED BY PLASTIC.

Panel 5: IRVING, DON'T YOU CARE IF I GO ON A TRIP BY MYSELF ON A STRANGE ISLAND FULL OF 40,000 ELIGIBLE BACHELORS?

NO. I THINK YOU'LL HAVE FUN.

Panel 6: AREN'T YOU AFRAID I'LL FALL MADLY IN LOVE WITH SOME GUY, SAIL AWAY ON HIS YACHT, AND FORGET ABOUT YOU COMPLETELY??

Panel 7: CATHY, IF YOU CAN FORGET ALL ABOUT ME IN 7 DAYS, THEN THERE OBVIOUSLY ISN'T THAT MUCH TO REMEMBER.

HOW CAN YOU SAY THAT, IRVING??

Panel 8: YOU'RE TAKING ALL THE FUN OUT OF MAKING YOU JEALOUS!!!

WHAT DO YOU MEAN, YOU THINK YOU'RE CANCELLING YOUR TRIP TO THE BAHAMAS, CATHY?!!

I'M JUST AFRAID OF BEING ALONE, ANDREA.

I'M AFRAID TO FLY ALONE... I'M AFRAID TO EAT ALONE... I'M AFRAID TO WALK THE STREETS ALONE... I'M AFRAID TO GO OUT ALONE...

CATHY, THE ONLY THING YOU'RE REALLY AFRAID OF IS DISCOVERING THAT YOU **CAN** MAKE IT YOURSELF!! YOU'RE JUST AFRAID OF YOURSELF!!

I NEVER THOUGHT OF THAT, ANDREA.

THAT MAKES ME A COMPLETE COWARD.

DON'T YOU WANT TO KNOW THE NUMBER WHERE I CAN BE REACHED ON MY VACATION, MR. PINKLEY?

NO, CATHY. JUST ENJOY YOURSELF.

DON'T YOU WANT ME TO TYPE OUT A MINUTE-BY-MINUTE INSTRUCTION SHEET FOR THE PERSON WHO'LL BE TAKING MY PLACE??

NO...WE CAN HANDLE IT.

DON'T YOU NEED ME HERE AT ALL, MR. PINKLEY??!!

CATHY, IT'S ONLY A VACATION. WE'LL GET ALONG FINE.

I HATE IT WHEN THE ONLY ONE WHO THINKS I'M INDISPENSABLE IS ME.

63

Panel 1:
YOU'RE TAKING ALL THIS FOR A ONE WEEK TRIP??

YEAH. IF I MEET SOME GUY WHO WANTS TO TAKE ME TO FANCY RESTAURANTS, I'LL NEED ALL MY BEST DRESSES.

Panel 2:
IF I MEET SOME GUY WHO LIKES TO SAIL, I'LL HAVE TO HAVE ALL MY BOAT CLOTHES... IF I MEET ...

Panel 3:
YOU'RE NOT SUPPOSED TO WORRY ABOUT THAT STUFF WHEN YOU'RE PACKING, CATHY!!!

YOU'RE RIGHT, ANDREA.

Panel 4:
I SHOULD WORRY ABOUT MEETING SOME GUY WHO CAN LIFT MY SUITCASES.

Panel 5:
DO YOU THINK CATHY WILL BE OKAY BY HERSELF IN THE BAHAMAS?

OF COURSE SHE WILL. CATHY'S A GROWN WOMAN.

Panel 6:
SHE LIVES BY HERSELF... SHE TAKES CARE OF HERSELF... YOUR DAUGHTER IS NOT A BABY ANYMORE!!!

FLORIDA
BAHAMAS
TOLEDO

Panel 7:
BYE, MOM AND DAD.

Panel 8:
HOWEVER, MY DAUGHTER IS.

EXCUSE ME, MA'AM, BUT YOUR CHILD JUST THREW HIS CHICKEN TETRAZZINI IN MY LAP AGAIN.

OH, HOWARD, YOU LITTLE RASCAL.

UM, EXCUSE ME AGAIN, BUT DO YOU THINK LITTLE HOWARD WILL SCREAM LIKE THAT FOR THE FULL 5 HOUR FLIGHT TO THE BAHAMAS?

OH NO... WE'LL JUST FIND SOMETHING FOR HIM TO DO.

EXCUSE ME ONCE MORE, BUT DO YOU THINK HOWARD COULD DO SOMETHING BESIDES EAT MY CIGARETTES?

CIGARETTES?! YOU CAN'T HAVE CIGARETTES HERE!!

WE NON-SMOKERS HAVE OUR RIGHTS, YOU KNOW!!

I CAN'T GO OUT THERE TO LIE IN THE SUN! ALL THOSE PEOPLE ARE ALREADY THIN AND TAN!

WHAT DO YOU EXPECT? THIS IS THE BAHAMAS.

CHANGING ROOMS

YEAH, BUT THE PEOPLE IN OUR TOUR GROUP AREN'T ALL THIN AND TAN! WHERE'S MY MORAL SUPPORT??

TO POOL

TOUR GUIDE

WHERE ARE ALL THE FAT, PALE PEOPLE I CAME HERE WITH ON THE AIRPLANE??!!

RELAX, CATHY. I'M SURE YOUR GROUP WILL BE ALONG SOON.

TOUR GUIDE

THERE ARE NEVER ANY FAT, PALE PEOPLE WHEN YOU NEED THEM.

6 FT.

Panel 1: HOW WAS YOUR LUNCH, CATHY? I SEE YOU HAD THE CONCH SHELL SOUP.

JUST FINE, THANKS.

Panel 2: OH GOOD. SO OFTEN WE FIND THAT YOUNG PEOPLE ON OUR BAHAMAS TOURS ARE A LITTLE NERVOUS ABOUT TRYING NEW THINGS.

Panel 3: THEY FIND IT DIFFICULT TO ENJOY EXPERIENCES OTHER THAN THOSE THEY'RE ALREADY FAMILIAR WITH.

OH, NOT ME. I'M READY FOR ANYTHING!!

Panel 4: WONDERFUL! WHAT DID YOU PLAN TO DO THIS AFTERNOON?

EAT DINNER.

Panel 5: I HAVE WANDERED DOWN MILES OF DAZZLING WHITE BEACH, AND NO GORGEOUS MAN WAS SPLASHING ALONG BESIDE ME, HOLDING MY HAND....

Panel 6: I HAVE FELT THE EVENING BREEZE BRUSH MY FACE, AND NO HANDSOME GUY WAS GAZING AT THE REFLECTION OF THE SUNSET IN MY EYES...

Panel 7: I HAVE EXPLORED THE MYSTERIES OF THE CORAL... I HAVE SIPPED THE JUICES OF THE TROPICS, AND NO 6'2" HUNK WAS AT MY SIDE...

Panel 8: I THINK I TAKE MY TRAVEL BROCHURES TOO SERIOUSLY.

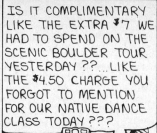

DON'T FORGET THE COMPLIMENTARY GOOMBAY COCKTAIL PARTY AT THE HOTEL POOL TONIGHT, CATHY.

COMPLIMENTARY?

IS IT COMPLIMENTARY LIKE THE EXTRA $7 WE HAD TO SPEND ON THE SCENIC BOULDER TOUR YESTERDAY ??...LIKE THE $4.50 CHARGE YOU FORGOT TO MENTION FOR OUR NATIVE DANCE CLASS TODAY ???

OH NO. THIS IS COMPLETELY FREE.

OH YEAH? WHAT DO YOU DO THERE ??

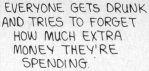

EVERYONE GETS DRUNK AND TRIES TO FORGET HOW MUCH EXTRA MONEY THEY'RE SPENDING.

MY MOTHER THINKS I'M TOURING BOTANICAL GARDENS, SIPPING FRUIT JUICE OUT OF COCONUT SHELLS WITH SOME ELIGIBLE, YET RESPECTFUL BACHELOR.

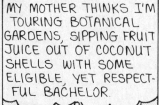

ANDREA THINKS I'M LOUNGING IN THE SUN, DISCUSSING THE E.R.A., WHILE SOME GORGEOUS GUY SMEARS PAPAYA OIL ON MY FEET.

IRVING THINKS I'M HITTING EVERY BAR AND DISCO IN THE BAHAMAS, DANCING AND DRINKING MY BRAINS OUT.

EVERYONE ALWAYS HAS A BETTER TIME ON MY VACATIONS THAN I DO.

67

MY SECRETARY, ALEX, HAS BEEN COMPLAINING ABOUT NOT BEING ABLE TO COPE WITH THE NEW ATTITUDES OF WOMEN... ...AND IT'S GIVEN ME AN IDEA, ANDREA.

I'M GOING TO START UP A CLASS THAT TEACHES MALE SURVIVAL.

CATHY, THAT'S **BRILLIANT** !!!

BY HELPING MEN LEARN HOW TO ADAPT TO HOW THINGS ARE CHANGING, YOU'LL BE HELPING ALL WOMEN REACH OUR GOAL OF EQUALITY !!!!

NOT TO MENTION MY GOAL OF BEING IN CHARGE OF A ROOMFUL OF GUYS.

THREE OF MY FRIENDS WANT TO JOIN THE MALE SURVIVAL CLASS YOU'RE STARTING, CATHY.

SEE, IRVING? MEN **DO** WANT TO LEARN TO TAKE CARE OF THEMSELVES !

THEY **DO** WANT TO FEEL THE SATISFACTION THAT COMES FROM MAKING THEIR KITCHENS GERM-FREE AND THEIR WASH APRIL FRESH !!

THEY DO WANT TO EXPERIENCE THE SPECIAL POWER A WOMAN HAS IN HER HOME !!!

THEY ALREADY HAVE, CATHY.

ALL THEIR GIRLFRIENDS THREATENED TO DUMP THEM IF THEY DIDN'T SIGN UP.

69

WELCOME TO MY CLASS ON MALE SURVIVAL. IN THIS FIRST SESSION, WE WILL LEARN TO IDENTIFY COMMON HOUSEHOLD ITEMS.

NOW, JIM, CAN YOU TELL ME WHAT THIS IS?

I THINK IT'S A BROOM.

IRVING??

A SEWING MACHINE??

ALEX???

A TRASH MASHER???

YOU DUMMIES, THIS IS AN IRON!!!

MALE SURVIVAL SEMINAR

5 OR 7 IRON?

MALE SURVIVAL SEMINAR

A CRUCIAL PART OF MALE SURVIVAL IS FOR MEN TO LEARN TO DO THEIR LAUNDRY ALL BY THEMSELVES.

MALE SURVIVAL SEMINAR

HERE WE HAVE PRE-SOAK, STAIN SPRAY, DETERGENT, BLEACH, FABRIC SOFTENER AND SPRAY STARCH.

MALE SURVIVAL SEMINAR

NOW, ALEX, **WITHOUT THE HELP** OF A GIRLFRIEND, A CLEANING LADY, A SISTER OR A LAUNDRY SERVICE... TELL THE CLASS WHAT YOU WOULD DO FIRST TO GET YOUR LAUNDRY DONE!!

CALL MY MOTHER.

MALE SURVIVAL SEMINAR

C'MON, IRVING. AS PART OF YOUR HOMEWORK FOR MY MALE SURVIVAL CLASS, YOU HAVE TO SCRUB THE FLOOR.

BUT CATHY, YOU DO IT SO MUCH **BETTER** THAN I DO.

OH NO YOU DON'T! YOU'RE NOT GOING TO FLATTER ME INTO DOING YOUR WORK FOR YOU AGAIN! .... AND WHY **SHOULD** YOU?

YOU'RE A BIG, STRONG MAN, IRVING. YOU COULD PROBABLY GET THIS FLOOR CLEAN IN **HALF** THE TIME THAT I COULD!!

OH YEAH??

WAIT A MINUTE.

THAT **DOES** IT, CATHY! I'M QUITTING YOUR MALE SURVIVAL CLASS!!

WHAT?!

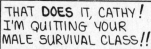

CATHY, I HAVE STABBED MYSELF WITH AN EMBROIDERY NEEDLE... ...I'VE BURNED MY ARM WITH A SOUFFLE PAN... ...I HAVE A RASH ON MY KNEE FROM SCOURING POWDER.....

...THE WASHING MACHINE TURNED ALL MY UNDERWEAR PINK.... AND MY LEFT FOOT IS WELDED TO THE FLOOR WITH MOP'N'GLOW!!!

SO YOU'RE **QUITTING??**

WHAT DO YOU **EXPECT** ME TO DO?!!!

START DINNER.

71

THIS MALE SURVIVAL CLASS WAS A GOOD IDEA, CATHY, BUT IT'S NOT GOING TO WORK.

GUYS JUST DON'T CARE AS MUCH AS LADIES ABOUT KEEPING THE HOUSE ALL NEAT AND CLEAN.

ALEX, THERE IS NO GENETIC DIFFERENCE THAT CAUSES A GUY TO **MAKE** A MESS AND A LADY TO **CLEAN** THE MESS UP!! IT'S CONDITIONING!!!

SO WHAT? WE STILL DON'T CARE.

THEN WHO DO YOU THINK **DID** THE CONDITIONING?!!

WELL, I HOPE YOU'RE SATISFIED. EVERY ONE OF YOU FLUNKED YOUR MALE SURVIVAL EXAM.

DO YOU GUYS **WANT** TO LIVE IN FILTHY HOUSES?! DO YOU **WANT** TO HAVE TO BRIBE YOUR MOTHERS TO WASH YOUR CLOTHES?! DO YOU **WANT** TO DEPEND ON YOUR GIRL-FRIENDS TO COOK YOUR SUPPERS?!!

DO YOU **WANT** TO BE CATERED TO FOR THE REST OF YOUR LIVES LIKE A BUNCH OF BABIES?!!!

YES!!!

I QUIT.

HOW COME YOU'RE NOT AT WORK TODAY CATHY? ARE YOU SICK?

NO, ANDREA. I JUST REALLY NEEDED TO STAY HOME.

I KNOW HOW YOU FEEL. YOU NEED TIME TO THINK...TO REANALYZE....

...TO PREPARE YOURSELF FOR THE IMPORTANT BUSINESS DECISIONS YOU HAVE TO MAKE.

NOT EXACTLY, ANDREA.

I COULDN'T FIGURE OUT WHAT TO WEAR.

HERE'S MY CHECK AND MY DRIVER'S LICENSE.

FINE. I'LL JUST NEED TWO MAJOR CREDIT CARDS FOR IDENTIFICATION.

WHAT FOR?? MY DRIVER'S LICENSE TELLS YOU EVERYTHING YOU NEED TO KNOW ABOUT ME!!

ISN'T THAT **ENOUGH**?!!

TIMES HAVE CHANGED, MISS.

WE NOW REQUIRE THREE PIECES OF PLASTIC TO ESTABLISH THE TRUTH.

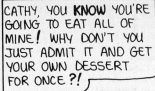

74

Panel 1:
IS BEING A SECRETARY GETTING YOU DOWN AGAIN, ALEX?
IT'S NOT JUST THAT, CATHY.

Panel 2:
EVERY CHICK I MEET HAS A BETTER PAYING JOB THAN MINE. THEY ALL HAVE CLASSIER CARS AND SLICKER APARTMENTS.

Panel 3:
EVERYTHING'S REVERSED, CATHY!! HOW AM I EVER SUPPOSED TO IMPRESS A LADY ANYMORE?!!!

Panel 4:
BETTER KEEP YOUR BODY IN GOOD SHAPE.

Panel 5:
YOU DON'T NEED THAT $50 OUTFIT, JOAN. WHITER TEETH AND FRESHER BREATH WILL GET GEORGE'S ATTENTION.

Panel 6:
I DON'T **BELIEVE** THAT COMMERCIAL!!
ME NEITHER.

Panel 7:
IF I DIDN'T BUY THE $50 OUTFIT, HE'D NEVER GET CLOSE ENOUGH TO NOTICE MY MOUTH.

I JUST DON'T FEEL LIKE A WORKING WOMAN, ANDREA. I FEEL LIKE A GIRL WITH A JOB.

YOU HAVE TO CHANGE YOUR IMAGE, CATHY.

GET A SASSY NEW HAIRDO... BUY SOME SLICK BUSINESSLIKE CLOTHES... DEVELOP A BRISK, CONFIDENT WALK....

REMODULATE YOUR VOICE SO IT'S STRONG AND SELF-ASSURED...

ANDREA, THIS ISN'T GOING TO MAKE ME FEEL LIKE A WORKING WOMAN.

I JUST RAN OUT OF TIME TO GO TO THE OFFICE.

BEFORE YOU GO HOME FOR THANKSGIVING, CATHY, I WANT TO ALERT YOU TO THE FACT THAT THIS IS THE MOST SEXIST HOLIDAY OF THE YEAR.

THE ENTIRE INSTITUTION IS BASED ON THE WOMEN SLAVING AWAY IN THE KITCHEN, WHILE THE MEN SAY "THANK YOU, SWEETIE" AND LOUNGE AROUND WATCHING FOOTBALL ON TV !!!!

I GUESS THAT'S WHY OUR FOREFATHERS NAMED IT THANKSGIVING.

YEAH...

...AND WHY OUR FOREMOTHERS NAMED IT TURKEY DAY.

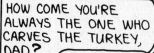

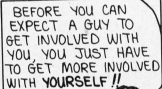

Panel 1: I JUST HAD A GREAT IDEA, ANDREA. I'M GOING TO HAVE A HALLOWEEN PARTY...

Panel 2: ...AND INVITE ALL THE MEN I'VE EVER HAD A REAL INTEREST IN SO I CAN MAKE IRVING JEALOUS!!

Panel 3: OH YEAH? WHO'S ON THE LIST?

Panel 4: SO FAR, I'VE GOT DAD AND GRANDPA.

Panel 5: WHAT KIND OF GAMES SHOULD I HAVE AT MY HALLOWEEN PARTY, IRVING?

GAMES?! CATHY, THAT'S FOR KIDS

Panel 6: WELL, WHAT ARE GROWN-UPS SUPPOSED TO DO AT PARTIES??

THEY'RE SUPPOSED TO STAND AROUND AND GET DRUNK SO THEY WON'T BE BORED.

Panel 7: THAT DOESN'T SOUND LIKE ANY FUN!!

SURE IT IS.

Panel 8: AFTER EVERYBODY GETS DRUNK, THEY START PLAYING GAMES.

WHERE'S YOUR HALLOWEEN CANDY, ANDREA?

I'M GIVING OUT GRANOLA THIS YEAR. IT'S BETTER FOR THE CHILDREN.

ANDREA, KIDS DON'T WANT TO TURN INTO HEALTH FREAKS ON HALLOWEEN! THEY WANT **CANDY**!!

THINK OF ALL THE DISAPPOINTED LITTLE FACES YOU'LL SEE WHEN YOU HAND OUT THAT STUFF!!

THE KIDS WILL GET PLENTY OF CANDY OTHER PLACES, CATHY.

THEN THINK OF **MY** DISAPPOINTED LITTLE FACE!!!

CREPE PAPER... APPLES... GOBLIN FACES... FAKE WORMS AND EYEBALLS... WITCHES... SKELETONS.....

405

I'VE GOT EVERY TRICK IN THE BOOK.

RING RING!

HI, CATHY. IT'S IRVING. SORRY, BUT I CAN'T MAKE IT TO YOUR HALLOWEEN PARTY.

...BUT NO TREAT.

HELLO, MY GORGEOUS DARLING. WHAT'S NEW?

I WANT YOU TO START GOING OUT WITH OTHER GIRLS MORE OFTEN, IRVING.

CATHY! YOU MEAN YOU FINALLY REALIZED HOW MUCH A GUY LIKE ME NEEDS HIS FREEDOM??!

NO. I FINALLY REALIZED HOW MUCH SWEETER YOU ARE WHEN YOU'RE FEELING GUILTY.

MMM.... YOU'RE SO SWEET.... YOU'RE SO GOOD...

...YOU'RE JUST WHAT I NEEDED TO MAKE THIS SATURDAY NIGHT COMPLETE.

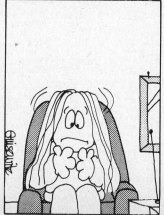

I THINK I'M HAVING A RELATIONSHIP WITH A BLUEBERRY PIE.

WHAT ARE YOU DOING, CATHY?

HOMEWORK FOR MY ADULT ED. COURSE.

I THOUGHT YOU SIGNED UP FOR MIND AND BODY AWARENESS!

I DID.

BUT AFTER THE FIRST NIGHT, I SWITCHED TO CAKE DECORATING.

WHAT??!

MY MIND BECAME AWARE THAT MY BODY WANTED CAKE.

WANT TO GO TO THE WOMEN AWAKE LECTURE WITH ME TONIGHT, CATHY?

I CAN'T ANDREA. I HAVE TO PRACTICE MAKING PETUNIA PETALS FOR MY CAKE DECORATING CLASS.

I DON'T BELIEVE THIS! DO YOU ACTUALLY WANT TO GIVE THIS MUCH OF YOUR LIFE OVER TO FROSTING???

DO YOU WANT TO HAVE YOUR WHOLE IDENTITY WRAPPED UP IN A CAKE FULL OF PINK CHIFFON PETUNIA PETALS?!!!?!

I THINK I ALREADY DO.

Panel 1: WHAT'S SO BAD ABOUT TAKING A CAKE DECORATING CLASS, ANDREA?

Panel 2: IT'S JUST STUPID, CATHY. THERE ARE SO MANY MORE CONSTRUCTIVE WAYS TO USE YOUR TIME.

Panel 3: YOU COULD BE IMPROVING YOUR MIND!! ENLIGHTENING OTHERS!! YOU COULD BE MAKING THE WORLD A BETTER PLACE TO LIVE!!!

Panel 4: I LIKE TO THINK I'M MAKING THE WORLD A BETTER PLACE TO EAT.

Panel 5: TA DA! IT'S MY DAD'S BIRTHDAY TODAY..... AND LOOK WHAT I MADE HIM!

WHAT IS IT?

Panel 6: IT'S MY FINAL PROJECT FOR MY CAKE DECORATING CLASS. SEE?... I HAVE A LAYER OF FROSTING FLOWERS FOR EVERY YEAR OF HIS BIRTHDAY.

Panel 7: GEE... HOW OLD IS YOUR DAD??

Panel 8: HE JUST TURNED 14.

89

C'MON, CATHY! THE HACKETTS' PARTY HAS BEEN GOING ON FOR 3 HOURS ALREADY!

FASTER, CATHY, FASTER! THE EXERCISE IS GOOD FOR YOU!!

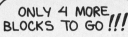
ONLY 4 MORE BLOCKS TO GO!!!

I FAIL TO SEE WHY YOU KEEP REFERRING TO THIS AS "FASHIONABLY" LATE.

HI CATHY. THIS IS EMERSON.

EMERSON??

YEA. REMEMBER ON OUR LAST DATE BACK IN JULY WHEN I ASKED WHEN I COULD SEE YOU AGAIN? YOU LAUGHED AND SAID, "HOW ABOUT SEPTEMBER 29?"...

WELL, THIS IS IT!!! THIS IS SEPTEMBER 29!

I HATE IT WHEN THE FUTURE COMES BACK TO HAUNT ME.

NO THANKS, EMERSON. NOT TONIGHT.

CATHY, FIVE MINUTES AGO, YOU WERE **PLEADING** FOR A CHANCE TO GO OUT TONIGHT !!

FIVE MINUTES AGO, YOU WERE CRYING ALL OVER THE APARTMENT BECAUSE NO ONE EVER CALLED YOU UP !!!

FIVE MINUTES AGO, YOU SAID YOU'D GIVE ANYTHING FOR A DATE WITH SOMEONE... ANYONE !!!

APPARENTLY, I'M PICKIER THAN I THOUGHT.

IRVING JUST DOESN'T APPRECIATE YOU THE WAY I DO, CATHY.

HE DOES TOO, EMERSON.

YEA?? WHAT DOES **HE** EVER SAY ABOUT HOW SWEET YOU ARE ?? **NOTHING !!**

WELL, **I** SAY YOU'RE NOT ONLY SWEET, BUT YOU'RE PRETTY AND SMART AND SENSITIVE AND SEXY AND...

HOW COME THE RIGHT WORDS ALWAYS COME OUT OF THE WRONG MOUTH ?

PLEASE DON'T ASK ME OUT AGAIN, EMERSON. IRVING AND I ARE **GOING TOGETHER**!

WHERE ARE YOU GOING?

WE'RE NOT GOING **ANYPLACE**, EMERSON. WE'RE GOING **TOGETHER**!!

CATHY, IF YOU'RE NOT GOING ANYPLACE, HOW CAN YOU BE GOING THERE TOGETHER?

WE'RE NOT!!

GOOD. WANNA GO OUT?

HOW WAS YOUR DATE WITH EMERSON LAST NIGHT, CATHY?

OKAY, IRVING. IT FEELS KIND OF DIFFERENT TO GO OUT WITH HIM.

WHAT'S DIFFERENT ABOUT IT??

YOU KNOW... HE HOLDS MY HAND, HE OPENS THE DOORS, HE PAYS MY WAY, HE.....

THAT'S SUPERFICIAL GARBAGE, CATHY! WHAT **FEELS** DIFFERENT?! HOW WOULD YOU FEEL IF YOU WERE OUT WITH THAT LITTLE TWERP TONIGHT INSTEAD OF ME?!!!

$7.50 RICHER.

TICKE

STAR WARS

92

93

I THINK EMERSON **DOES** APPRECIATE ME MORE, IRVING. MAYBE YOU AND I SHOULD JUST FORGET IT.

HOW CAN YOU SAY THAT, CATHY?! YOU DO MY LAUNDRY FOR ME....YOU COOK DINNER FOR ME SOMETIMES....

YOU WASH MY CAR BETTER THAN ANYONE.....YOU ALWAYS REMEMBER TO PICK UP SOME BEER FOR ME ON YOUR WAY OVER....

CATHY, YOU NEED ME !!!

WELL, ANDREA. I'VE WRITTEN TO ALL THE ADVICE COLUMNS I COULD FIND, AND THE SCORES ARE IN.

14 SAY I SHOULD GIVE EMERSON A CHANCE AND ONE SAYS I SHOULD STICK IT OUT WITH IRVING.

I DON'T BELIEVE THIS, CATHY!

WHY DON'T YOU ASK **YOURSELF** FOR THE ANSWER?! WHY CAN'T YOU LOOK INSIDE **YOUR-SELF** AND FIND OUT HOW **YOU** REALLY FEEL?!!

I ALREADY TRIED THAT, ANDREA.

HOW ELSE DO YOU THINK IRVING GOT HIS VOTE.

94

LET'S TALK ABOUT WHAT'S BUGGING YOU, CATHY.

NOTHING'S BUGGING ME TODAY, IRVING.

SO? LET'S TALK.

HOW COME YOU ONLY WANT TO HAVE THESE SERIOUS DISCUSSIONS WHEN I'M HAPPY?!!

WHERE ARE YOU ON THE DAYS THAT I'M DEPRESSED?! WHERE ARE YOU WHEN I'M LONELY AND DEJECTED?! IRVING, WHERE ARE YOU WHEN I'M MAD?!

HELLO?... IRVING?...

IT DOESN'T LOOK LIKE I'LL EVER GET MARRIED, ANDREA.

WELL, THERE'S NO HURRY.

YOU NEED TO PURSUE YOUR OWN INTERESTS FIRST, CATHY! YOU NEED TO DISCOVER WHAT ELSE YOU CAN DO!

YOU NEED A CAREER FIRST, AND THEN A MARRIAGE!...DON'T YOU SEE WHAT THAT WILL MEAN TO YOUR LIFE?!!

YEA. ABOUT A 10 YEAR WAIT BEFORE I CAN GET MY GOOD CHINA.

95

WELCOME ONCE AGAIN TO PEOPLE'S BANK AND TRUST... WHERE PEOPLE MAKE THE DIFFERENCE.

I WOULD LIKE ONE OF YOUR PEOPLE TO MAKE THE DIFFERENCE BE- TWEEN THE $233.00 I SAY I HAVE IN MY ACCOUNT AND THE 17¢ YOU SAY I HAVE !!

OH, WELL, OUR PEOPLE CAN'T MAKE THAT KIND OF DIFFERENCE... WE MAKE THE DIFFERENCE WITH OUR CHEERFUL SERVICE!

WELL, NO WONDER YOU'RE CHEERFUL.

YOU HAVE ALL THE MONEY !!!

HOW DID THINGS WORK OUT AT THE BANK, CATHY?

THEY WON, ANDREA. THE BANK ALWAYS WINS.

WELL, DON'T YOU FEEL BETTER FOR HAVING PUT UP A FIGHT?

NO, ANDREA. I FEEL STUPID. I MADE A BIG FUSS, AND IT TURNED OUT THAT I'D BEEN WRONG ALL ALONG.

EVERYTIME I MAKE A BIG FUSS ABOUT SOMETHING, IT TURNS OUT THAT I WAS WRONG !!!

NO, CATHY. YOU'RE WRONG ABOUT THAT.

Panel 1: I'M DOING IT! I'M FINALLY PROVING I'M NOT EMBARRASSED TO GO OUT TO DINNER BY MYSELF ANYMORE!

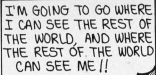

Panel 2: I'M GOING TO GO WHERE I CAN SEE THE REST OF THE WORLD, AND WHERE THE REST OF THE WORLD CAN SEE ME!!

Panel 3: HELLO. DINNER FOR ONE, PLEASE!

ONE? RIGHT THIS WAY.

Panel 4: I HAVE A NICE LITTLE TABLE TUCKED AWAY OVER HERE IN THE CORNER.

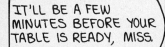

Panel 5: IT'LL BE A FEW MINUTES BEFORE YOUR TABLE IS READY, MISS.

CAN'T I SIT AT ONE OF THE EMPTY TABLES OVER THERE?

Panel 6: OH NO. WE HAVE TO SAVE THOSE FOR OUR LARGER PARTIES.

BUT THERE AREN'T ANY LARGER PARTIES! I'M THE ONLY ONE HERE.

Panel 7: AH, BUT IF A LARGER PARTY COMES, WE HAVE TO HAVE A TABLE AVAILABLE RIGHT AWAY.

FOR WHAT??

Panel 8: WHY, WE COULDN'T KEEP ALL THOSE OTHER PEOPLE WAITING.

OH, MISS... MISS? MAY I PLEASE SEE THE MENU?

OH, MISS... MISS? FORGET THE MENU. I'LL JUST ORDER.

OH, MISS... FORGET ABOUT DINNER. I JUST HAVE TIME FOR COFFEE NOW!

FORGET EVERYTHING, MISS! **THIS SERVICE IS JUST TERRIBLE!!**

WHAT DO YOU EXPECT WHEN YOU KEEP CHANGING YOUR MIND?

WHAT HAPPENED TO YOUR NEW PROGRAM OF TAKING YOURSELF OUT TO DINNER, CATHY?

I GAVE IT UP, ANDREA.

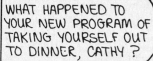

I'M JUST GOING TO SIT IN FRONT OF MY TV SET WHERE I CAN EAT IN PEACE AND QUIET.

NOBODY BOTHERS ME HERE! NOBODY TALKS TO ME! NOBODY HASSLES ME!!

WHAT WAS SO BAD ABOUT EATING OUT ALONE?

NOBODY PAID ANY ATTENTION TO ME.

Panel 1: I JUST LOVE THIS NEW LABELING THEY PUT ON EVERYTHING, ANDREA.

Panel 2: I USED TO THINK THIS STUFF WAS REAL FATTENING, AND HERE IT SAYS IT ONLY HAS 88 CALORIES PER SERVING.

Panel 3: CATHY, IT ALSO SAYS THERE ARE SUPPOSED TO BE 20 SERVINGS PER PACKAGE.

Panel 4: I HATE THIS STUPID LABELING.

Panel 5: PLEASE DON'T DRAG ME TO ANOTHER ONE OF YOUR SELF-IMPROVEMENT CLASSES, ANDREA.

I CAN'T HELP IT, CATHY.

Panel 6: I CAN'T STAND TO SEE YOU BEING SO NEGATIVE ABOUT YOURSELF ALL THE TIME.

Panel 7: YOU NEED SOMETHING TO REALLY HELP YOU REALIZE THAT YOU'RE A PERFECT HUMAN BEING JUST EXACTLY AS YOU ARE.

Panel 8: IF I'M SO PERFECT, WHAT DO I NEED TO GO TO ANOTHER SELF-IMPROVEMENT CLASS FOR?

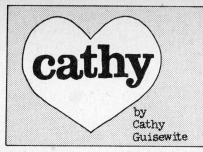

cathy

by
Cathy
Guisewite

HOW MANY IN YOUR PARTY, MISS?

JUST ONE.

HOW MANY IN YOUR PARTY, SIR?

JUST ONE.

WOW. THAT GUY IS REALLY CUTE.

THAT GIRL IS ADORABLE.

I WISH I COULD THINK OF SOMETHING WITTY TO SAY TO INTRODUCE MYSELF.

I'D LOVE TO MEET HER, BUT I DON'T WANT TO JUST HAND HER SOME DUMB LINE.

WELL, HE'S NOT LOOKING AT ME ANYMORE, SO I GUESS HE'S NOT INTERESTED.

I'M SURE SHE HAS A BOYFRIEND, ANYWAY.

ACTUALLY, HIS SUIT IS A LITTLE TACKY AND I BET HE'S WEARING HIS SOCKS INSIDE OUT.

ON SECOND THOUGHT, I NEVER COULD STAND GIRLS WHO BITE THEIR FINGERNAILS.

I BET HE HAS PURPLE POLYESTER SHAG CARPETING IN HIS BATHROOM, AND THAT THE ONLY THING SICKER THAN HIS SENSE OF HUMOR IS HIS BORING DISPOSITION.

I HATE GIRLS WITH STRINGY HAIR AND FLAT FEET.

BLEEACKK!!

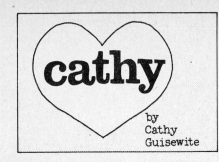

cathy

by Cathy Guisewite

ARE YOU GOING TO CHANGE YOUR NAME, ANDREA?

WHY WOULD I WANT TO CHANGE MY NAME?

YOU KNOW, WHEN YOU GET MARRIED.

WHY WOULD I WANT TO GET MARRIED?

WELL, I CAN UNDERSTAND WHY A WOMAN WOULD WANT TO KEEP HER LAST NAME WHEN SHE GETS MARRIED TO RETAIN HER IDENTITY, ANDREA,... BUT IT JUST ISN'T GOING TO WORK.

OF COURSE IT IS, CATHY.

NO IT ISN'T. IF HER HUSBAND KEEPS HIS LAST NAME TOO, WHAT'LL THEY CALL THE KIDS?

SIMPLE. LOTS OF COUPLES JUST GIVE THEIR CHILDREN BOTH NAMES... LIKE "SUSAN ANNE WILSON-CARPENTER."

YEAH, WELL, IF "SUSAN ANNE WILSON-CARPENTER" WANTS TO MARRY A GUY NAMED "GEORGE WILLIAM YOUNGMARK-ROBERTS," WHAT WILL THEY CALL THEIR KIDS?

EASY. THEY JUST COMBINE THE NAMES AGAIN.

ANDREA, THAT MEANS SOME POOR LITTLE KID WOULD HAVE A NAME LIKE "HEATHER LOUISE WILSON-CARPENTER-YOUNGMARK-ROBERTS" ...AND IF HEATHER EVER GOT MARRIED, HER DAUGHTER WOULD BE "MICHELLE JANE WILSON-CARPENTER-YOUNGMARK-ROBERTS-FRANKLIN-JONES-TURNER-LEWIS."

ANDREA, SOMEWHERE ALONG THE LINE, SOMEONE'S GOING TO HAVE TO BREAK DOWN AND GIVE UP PART OF THEIR IDENTITY!!

WHAT FOR?

IN ABOUT 5 GENERATIONS, THERE'S ONLY GOING TO BE ROOM FOR ONE PERSON IN THE PHONE BOOK.

Guisewite

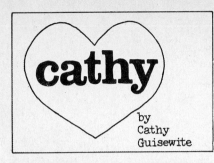

cathy

by
Cathy
Guisewite

CAN I HELP YOU?

I HOPE SO. I WANT TO GET A GREAT MOTHER'S DAY PRESENT

FINE. I HAPPEN TO HAVE JUST THE THING.

YOU WANT THE FRY-BABY FRYER OR THE CROCK POT?

NO... I DON'T THINK YOU UNDERSTAND... I WANT MY MOTHER'S DAY PRESENT TO BE REALLY SPECIAL.

I WANT A GIFT THAT REALLY SUMS UP HOW MUCH I APPRECIATE ALL THE YEARS OF UNSELFISH DEVOTION MY MOM HAS GIVEN ME.

I WANT A GIFT THAT'S WARM AND THOUGHTFUL... THAT TELLS HER HOW IMPORTANT SHE IS TO ME.

I WANT A GIFT THAT SAYS "I LOVE YOU".. "I ADMIRE YOU".. "I NEED YOU"!!

I WANT A GIFT THAT WILL FINALLY EXPRESS ALL THE THINGS I CAN NEVER QUITE PUT INTO WORDS!!

YES, I SEE. MAYBE EDNA HERE CAN HELP YOU WHILE I GO ON MY BREAK.

SHE'S TRYING TO DECIDE BETWEEN THE FRY-BABY FRYER AND THE CROCK POT.

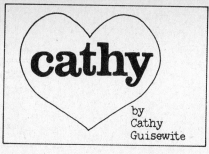

cathy

by Cathy Guisewite

C'MON, IRVING.

NOT NOW, CATHY.

BUT IRVING, WE HAVE TO TALK!!

NOT NOW, CATHY.

BUT IRVING, IN ORDER TO HAVE AN OPEN, GOOD RELATIONSHIP, WE HAVE TO TELL EACH OTHER HOW WE TRULY FEEL!

OKAY, CATHY, YOU ASKED FOR IT.

I FEEL ANNOYED THAT YOU WOULD BRING THIS UP WITH ONLY 14 SECONDS LEFT TO PLAY IN A GAME I'VE WAITED ALL WEEK TO SEE.

I FEEL FRUSTRATED THAT THE STAR PLAYER HAS JUST BEEN BUMPED FROM THE GAME FOR A FOUL I MISSED BECAUSE I WAS LISTENING TO YOU!

I FEEL NERVOUS AND ANGRY BECAUSE I HAPPEN TO HAVE 50 BUCKS RIDING ON THE TEAM THAT NOW HAS TO MAKE SPORTS HISTORY TO KEEP FROM LOSING!!!

HOW DO YOU FEEL??!!

FINE, THANKS.

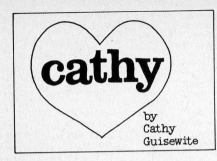

cathy

by Cathy Guisewite

"YOU BROUGHT YOUR SUIT, DIDN'T YOU?"

"NO. I'M BOYCOTTING, REMEMBER?"

"I THOUGHT YOU'D CHANGE YOUR MIND WHEN THE BEACH OPENED."

"HAH."

KEEP OUR PARK CLEAN

"YOU'RE ACTUALLY BOYCOTTING BATHING SUITS THIS YEAR, CATHY?"

"YES I AM, ANDREA. THEY JUST DON'T MAKE SENSE TO ME."

◄ PICNIC AREA
BEACH ►

"WE SPEND THE WHOLE WINTER TRYING TO FIGHT OFF GUYS WHO WANT TO REMOVE PART OF OUR CLOTHING..."

"...AND THEN WHEN MEMORIAL DAY COMES, WE'RE SUPPOSED TO JUST RIP OFF OUR CLOTHES OURSELVES AND GO ROMPING AROUND IN A BATHING SUIT THAT'S SKIMPIER THAN UNDERWEAR."

"WHY SHOULD WE DO THAT, ANDREA??"

"WHY SHOULD WE SUDDENLY WANT TO SHOW OFF WHAT WE'VE SPENT THE WHOLE REST OF THE YEAR TRYING TO NOT LET ANYONE ELSE SEE???"

"WELL, BRAVO, CATHY!! WHEN DID YOU DEVELOP SUCH STRONG PRINCIPLES?"

"SHORTLY AFTER I LOOKED AT MYSELF IN MY BATHING SUIT YESTERDAY."

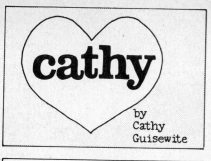

cathy

by
Cathy
Guisewite

WANT TO ORDER A PIZZA?

OKAY.

I'LL FIND THE PHONE NUMBER, YOU FIND THE PHONE.

WHERE'S YOUR PHONE BOOK, CATHY?

I DON'T KNOW, ANDREA. I'LL JUST CALL INFORMATION FOR THE NUMBER.

HELLO. THIS IS A RECORDING. AT THE MOMENT, ALL OUR INFORMATION LINES ARE BUSY.

WE AT THE PHONE COMPANY SINCERELY HOPE YOU'LL USE THE 5 TO 10 MINUTES YOU MAY HAVE TO WAIT FOR A FREE OPERATOR TO CHECK YOUR LOCAL DIRECTORY FOR THE LISTING YOU SEEK.

WE REGRET ANY INCONVENIENCE WE MAY BE CAUSING, BUT THEN, WHY DO YOU THINK WE PRINTED THAT BIG ... PHONE BOOK FOR YOU??

MAYBE NEXT TIME YOU'LL CONSIDER THE FACT THAT WE HAVE NEITHER THE TIME NOR THE MONEY TO LOOK UP PHONE NUMBERS FOR EVERY LOUSY PERSON IN THE WORLD WHO IS TOO LAZY TO DO IT HIMSELF!!

WHAT HAPPENED, CATHY?

THE RECORDING GOT MAD AND HUNG UP ON ME.

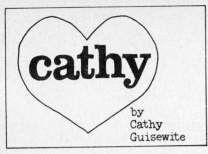

cathy

by Cathy Guisewite

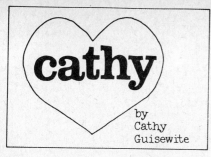

cathy

by
Cathy
Guisewite

HAPPY FATHER'S DAY, DAD!

THANKS, CATHY. WE WERE JUST LOOKING AT SOME OLD PICTURES

UH, OH.

OH, CATHY, YOU WERE SUCH A CUTE BABY. WE COULD TELL RIGHT AWAY THAT YOU HAD YOUR FATHER'S DISHWATER-BROWN EYES.

HAPPY FATHER'S DAY!!

AND HERE YOU ARE WHEN YOU WERE 2. SEE? EVEN THEN, YOU HAD YOUR FATHER'S FAT LITTLE CHEEKS

FATHER'S AY!!

OF COURSE, I'LL NEVER FORGET THE DAY YOU SPRAY-PAINTED THE REFRIGERATOR WHEN YOU WERE 5. YOU ALWAYS GOT IN TROUBLE FOR HAVING YOUR FATHER'S SENSE OF HUMOR.

YOU HAD YOUR FATHER'S TEMPER, TOO. HERE YOU ARE, GETTING SPANKED AT AGES 6, 8, AND 9.

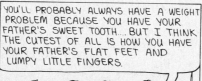

YOU'LL PROBABLY ALWAYS HAVE A WEIGHT PROBLEM BECAUSE YOU HAVE YOUR FATHER'S SWEET TOOTH.... BUT I THINK THE CUTEST OF ALL IS HOW YOU HAVE YOUR FATHER'S FLAT FEET AND LUMPY LITTLE FINGERS.

PY FATHER'S DAY!!

ALL THINGS CONSIDERED, SHOULDN'T I BE GETTING A PRESENT TODAY, TOO?

Y FATHER'S DAY!!

WOW! I LOST 3 POUNDS SINCE YESTERDAY!!

SINCE YESTERDAY? IT'S PROBABLY JUST WATER.

HAH! THAT JUST PROVES HOW LITTLE YOU KNOW ABOUT DIETING, ANDREA.

WHEN YOU **GAIN** 3 POUNDS, IT'S WATER.

WHEN YOU **LOSE** 3 POUNDS, IT'S WEIGHT.

WHEN I WAS LITTLE, I PUT MY OWN NEEDS FIRST, AND EVERYONE SAID I WAS BEING SELFISH AND INCONSIDERATE.

ICE CREAM

NOW EVERYONE SAYS I'M **SUPPOSED** TO PUT MY OWN NEEDS FIRST.

THAT'S RIGHT, CATHY.

PUTTING YOUR OWN NEEDS FIRST IS ONE OF THE MOST IMPORTANT THINGS YOU CAN DO TO MAINTAIN YOUR SELF-RESPECT.

HOW CAN I HAVE ANY SELF-RESPECT IF I'M BEING SELFISH AND INCONSIDERATE?

OF COURSE I'M NOT GOING TO QUIZ YOU ABOUT EVERY LITTLE DETAIL OF YOUR DATE LAST NIGHT, CATHY.

I JUST WANT TO KNOW THAT YOU'RE USING YOUR COMMON SENSE.

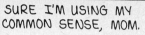

SURE I'M USING MY COMMON SENSE, MOM.

I ALSO WANT TO KNOW IF YOUR COMMON SENSE IS STILL THE SAME AS MY COMMON SENSE.

YOU JUST DON'T UNDERSTAND, ANDREA. WHEN IRVING ISN'T HERE, I MISS ALL THE LITTLE THINGS HE DOES FOR ME.

CATHY, IRVING DOESN'T DO **ANYTHING** FOR YOU !!

I MISS ALL THE LITTLE THINGS HE DOESN'T DO.

DEPOSIT $500 IN A NEW ACCOUNT HERE, AND YOU GET YOUR CHOICE OF A FREE ELECTRIC RAZOR OR ALARM CLOCK.

DEPOSIT $5000 AND YOU CAN CHOOSE BETWEEN A FREE PORTABLE MIXER OR ELECTRIC CAN OPENER.

ARE YOU CRAZY??

CERTAINLY NOT. IT'S OUR LITTLE WAY OF ENCOURAGING YOU TO TRUST YOUR MONEY TO US.

WHY WOULD I TRUST MY MONEY TO SOMEONE WHO THINKS THERE'S A $4500 DIFFERENCE BETWEEN AN ALARM CLOCK AND A CAN OPENER?

IF PEOPLE WERE SUPPOSED TO WEAR TOE NAIL POLISH, WE WOULD HAVE BEEN BORN WITH OUR FEET CLOSER TO OUR FACES.

Panel 1: YOU'RE LOOKING AT AN ALL NEW EMERSON, CATHY. I HAVE OVERCOME MY FEAR OF REJECTION, AND I'M READY TO GO INTRODUCE MYSELF TO THE LADY OF MY DREAMS.

disco tonigh

Panel 2: YOU ARE?

YES, CATHY. IN THE PAST 24 HOURS, I HAVE DEVELOPED NERVE OF STEEL!

disco tonig

Panel 3: I HAVE DEVELOPED A WILL OF IRON!!

WELL, GO GET'EM, EMERSON.

Panel 4: MY TONGUE JUST TURNED TO CEMENT.

Panel 5: LAST WEEK I TOOK A GIRL OUT AND SHE SLAPPED MY FACE BECAUSE I OPENED THE DOOR FOR HER.

Panel 6: THIS WEEK I TOOK ANOTHER GIRL OUT AND SHE SLAPPED MY FACE BECAUSE I **DIDN'T** OPEN THE DOOR FOR HER.

Panel 7: HOW'S A GUY SUPPOSED TO KNOW HOW TO ACT ANYMORE, CATHY??!

JUST LET THE GIRL YOU'RE WITH KNOW YOU RESPECT HER AS AN EQUAL BY TREATING HER AS AN EQUAL, EMERSON.

Panel 8: WHAT AM I SUPPOSED TO DO, SLAP HER BACK?

EVERY NIGHT I DRIVE HERE THINKING I'M GOING TO BE SO COOL AND SUAVE WITH THE LADIES... AND THEN I JUST SIT HERE RIPPING UP MY NAPKIN.

EVERYBODY DOES THAT, EMERSON.

EVERYONE'S INTIMIDATED BY A SINGLE'S BAR.

THOSE GUYS AREN'T. THEY'RE ALL JOKING AND GESTURING WITH THEIR DRINKS!

WHY CAN'T I EVER JOKE AND GESTURE WITH MY DRINK ??

I DON'T KNOW, EMERSON. JUST **DO** IT !!

I CAN'T. MY GLASS IS FULL OF PAPER.

EMERSON! WHAT ARE YOU DOING, SITTING HERE LAUGHING ALL BY YOURSELF ??

I'M PRETENDING LIKE I'M HAVING FUN.

I'VE NOTICED THAT THE WOMEN IN PLACES LIKE THIS ARE ALWAYS ATTRACTED TO THE MEN WHO LOOK LIKE THEY'RE HAVING FUN.

EMERSON, IF YOU WANT TO MEET SOMEONE, WHY DON'T YOU JUST GO INTRODUCE YOURSELF ??

IT DOESN'T WORK THAT WAY, CATHY.

AS SOON AS YOU START TALKING, EVERYBODY THINKS YOU'RE BEING A PHONEY.

THE FIRST DAY IN THE SUN, MY NOSE GOT PINK... ... AND MY LEGS STAYED WHITE.

THE SECOND DAY, MY NOSE GOT BRIGHT RED.. ... AND MY LEGS STAYED WHITE.

NOW MY NOSE IS SO SUNBURNED IT'S PRACTICALLY PURPLE... ... AND MY LEGS ARE STILL COMPLETELY WHITE.

HOW CAN THE SUN KEEP PASSING UP SOMETHING SO BIG TO GET TO SOMETHING SO LITTLE?

I CAN'T BELIEVE IT, ANDREA. IT'S THE 4TH OF JULY, AND I'M STILL FAT.

IF I'D JUST STAYED ON MY DIET SINCE THE BEGINNING OF SUMMER, I'D BE THIN AND GORGEOUS BY NOW. IF I'D...

CATHY, THE PAST IS PAST.

JUST START YOUR DIET TODAY AND THINK HOW GREAT YOU'LL FEEL BY THE END OF SUMMER.

IT'LL NEVER WORK, ANDREA.

THE ONLY TIME I'VE EVER SUCCEEDED ON A DIET IS IN RETROSPECT.

117

HOW ABOUT SOME OF THIS NEW PERFUME? IT HAS A DIFFERENT FRAGRANCE ON EVERY GIRL WHO WEARS IT.

IT REALLY BRINGS OUT THE BEST IN YOU, AND BECOMES YOUR OWN, INDIVIDUAL SCENT.

IF I DON'T LIKE THE PERFUME, AM I SUPPOSED TO RETURN IT OR ME?

HI. COULD YOU CUT THIS ROAST IN HALF FOR ME?

SORRY...WE CAN'T CUT IT ONCE IT'S WRAPPED.

RING BELL FOR SERVICE

WELL, COULD YOU CUT A NEW ROAST FOR ME THAT'S A LITTLE SMALLER?

SORRY...ALL THE ROASTS WE'VE GOT ARE ALREADY OUT.

WELL, COULD YOU COME OUT AND HELP ME FIND A SMALLER ROAST??

OH NO, MISS. I HAVE TO STAY BEHIND THE COUNTER.

RING BELL FOR SERVICE

WHAT IF SOMEONE CAME ALONG AND NEEDED SOME HELP?

119

WHERE DID YOU GET THIS SINGLE GRAPEFRUIT... THEY'RE SUPPOSED TO COME IN BAGS OF 12.

I TOOK IT OUT OF THE BAG.

MISS, IF YOU SINGLE PEOPLE WANT TO SHOP AT A SUPERMARKET, YOU'LL JUST HAVE TO GET USED TO SUPERMARKET **QUANTITIES**!!

DO YOU EXPECT TO BUY **ONE CARROT, TOO?!** ONE BOWL OF CORNFLAKES?!!

OKAY, OKAY. FORGET THE GRAPEFRUIT. I'LL JUST TAKE THESE FROZEN PIZZAS YOU'VE GOT ON SALE.

SORRY. LIMIT ONE PER CUSTOMER.

YOU WANT TO BUY **3 SINGLE EGGS ???** MISS, EGGS DO NOT COME SINGLY. THEY'RE SOLD BY THE DOZEN.

SAYS WHO?? DO THE CHICKENS **LAY** 12 EGGS AT ONCE?! DO YOU THINK ANYONE **EATS** 12 EGGS AT ONCE??!!

WHY DO I HAVE TO BUY 12 EGGS JUST BECAUSE THAT'S HOW THE CARTONS ARE MADE?!!!

WHY ARE YOU BUYING THAT PACKAGE OF 12 CANDY BARS??

THEY CAME THAT WAY.

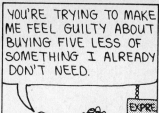

FIRST IRVING SAID HE HATED THE WAY I MUSH UP MY ICE CREAM BEFORE I EAT IT... AND THEN I SAID THAT ANYONE WHO LIKES PINEAPPLE SUNDAES IS STUPID.

THEN IRVING SCREAMED AT ME FOR NOT FIGURING THE TIP OUT IN ONE SECOND, AND I SHOUTED AT HIM FOR WADDING UP HIS NAPKIN ON HIS PLATE.

WAIT A MINUTE, CATHY. THIS DOESN'T SOUND LIKE A VERY SERIOUS FIGHT TO ME.

ARE YOU KIDDING?

THE BIGGER THE FIGHT, THE LITTLER THE THINGS WE YELL AT EACH OTHER ABOUT.

THEY PLAY MUSIC IN THE GROCERY STORE SO YOU'LL BE HAPPY WHILE YOU SPEND ALL YOUR MONEY.

THEY PLAY MUSIC IN THE DENTIST'S OFFICE, SO YOU'LL BE HAPPY WHILE YOUR MOUTH IS BEING DRILLED TO PIECES.

AND NOW THEY PLAY MUSIC OVER THE PHONE, SO YOU'LL BE HAPPY WHILE YOU WAIT FOR 15 MINUTES TO TALK TO SOMEONE.

ALL OF THE SUDDEN, I CAN'T GET MAD WITHOUT HEARING VIOLINS.

WHAT'S WRONG WITH HOW I ACTED AT THE PARTY, CATHY?

YOU TALKED ABOUT YOURSELF THE WHOLE TIME, IRVING.

YOU NEVER TALKED ABOUT **US**!

YOU NEVER LAUGHED AND MENTIONED SOME CUTE LITTLE THING THAT I DO!

WHAT CUTE LITTLE THING DO YOU DO?

WHAT'S WRONG WITH SPENDING THE EVENING READING MY DIARY, ANDREA?

PLENTY, CATHY.

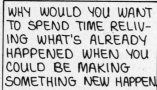

WHY WOULD YOU WANT TO SPEND TIME RELIVING WHAT'S ALREADY HAPPENED WHEN YOU COULD BE MAKING SOMETHING NEW HAPPEN?

WHY SINK BACK INTO THE PAST WHEN YOU COULD BE DOING SOMETHING FOR THE FUTURE??!

I LIKE THE PAST BETTER, ANDREA.

I'VE ALREADY BEEN THERE.

WHAT DO YOU WANT FOR CHRISTMAS, ANDREA?

I WANT TO BE A TRUE EQUAL IN EVERY WAY TO EVERY MAN!

C'MON, ANDREA... I CAN'T GIVE YOU THAT!

WHAT DO YOU REALLY WANT??

I WANT TO BE BETTER.

I DON'T THINK I CAN COME TO YOUR CHRISTMAS PARTY TONIGHT, ANDREA.

WHY NOT, CATHY??

WELL, I DECIDED I SHOULD SAMPLE ALL THE HORS D'OEUVRES I MADE RIGHT NOW, SO I WOULDN'T EMBARRASS MYSELF BY BEING A PIG AT YOUR PARTY LATER ON.

DON'T TELL ME....NOW YOU'RE SICK TO YOUR STOMACH.

NO, ANDREA. MY STOMACH'S FINE.

BUT IN THE LAST THREE HOURS, THE REST OF ME SEEMS TO HAVE OUTGROWN MY DRESS.